LIVING THINGS

HUMAN
BODY PARTS

BY

STEFFI CAVELL-CLARKE

©2017
Book Life
King's Lynn
Norfolk PE30 4LS

ISBN: 978-1-78637-077-8

Written by:
Steffi Cavell-Clarke

Edited by:
Grace Jones

Designed by:
Drue Rintoul

CONTENTS

Words that look like **this** can be found in the glossary on page 24.

WHAT IS A HUMAN BEING?

Planet Earth is home to many living things. All living things need water, air and sunlight to grow and survive. Animals, plants and humans are all living things.

A BOY IS A LIVING THING.

A BOOK IS A NON-LIVING THING.

A SUNFLOWER IS A LIVING THING.

4

Human beings live all over the world. You are a human being! Each human being is unique, which means we are all different from one another. Even though we might look different, we all share the same body parts.

HUMAN BODY PARTS

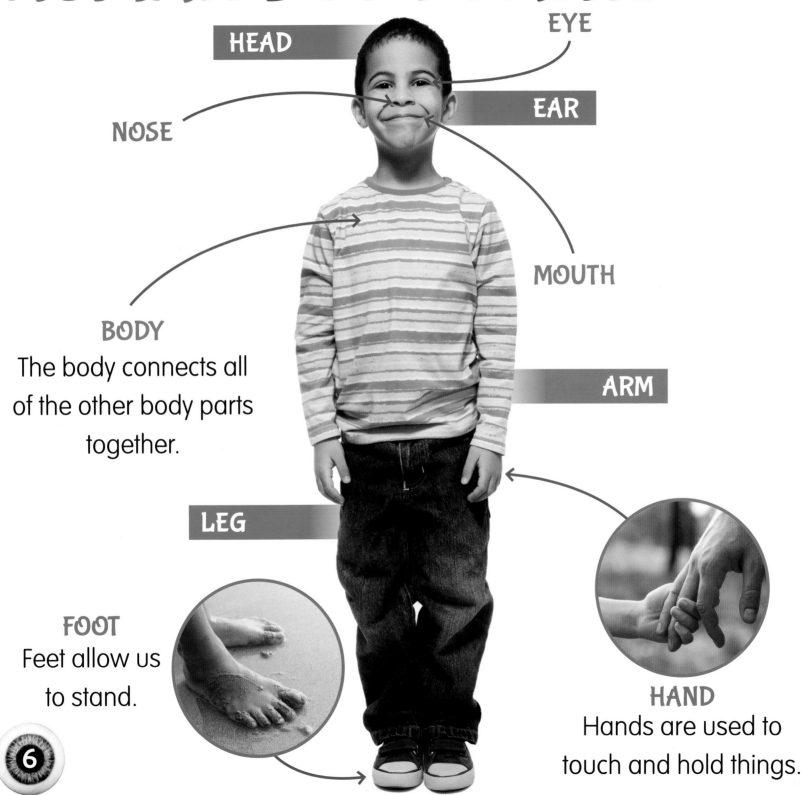

HEAD

EYE

NOSE

EAR

MOUTH

BODY
The body connects all of the other body parts together.

ARM

LEG

FOOT
Feet allow us to stand.

HAND
Hands are used to touch and hold things.

Arms can reach out towards things and help you to balance.

Legs support the body and allow us to walk, run and jump.

The head is an important part of the body. It is where the eyes, nose, mouth and ears are.

MUSCLES AND BONES

Underneath your skin are hundreds of bones and muscles. All of your bones connect to make up your skeleton. Your skeleton protects all of the **organs** inside your body, such as the heart.

SKELETON

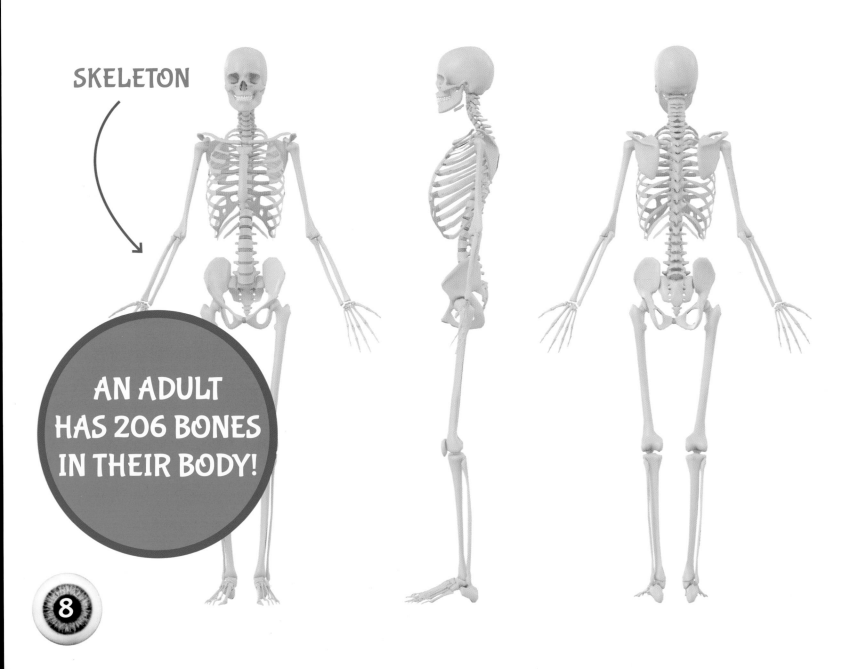

AN ADULT HAS 206 BONES IN THEIR BODY!

Your body can move because of your muscles. Muscles are made of **body tissue,** which are connected to bones by **tendons**. You use your muscles to move the bones in your body. Muscles that are used a lot often grow bigger and stronger.

YOUR HEART IS A MUSCLE!

HEAD

Your neck connects your head to your body. Your head protects your brain, which is an organ. The brain is like an amazing machine which allows you to think, learn and move.

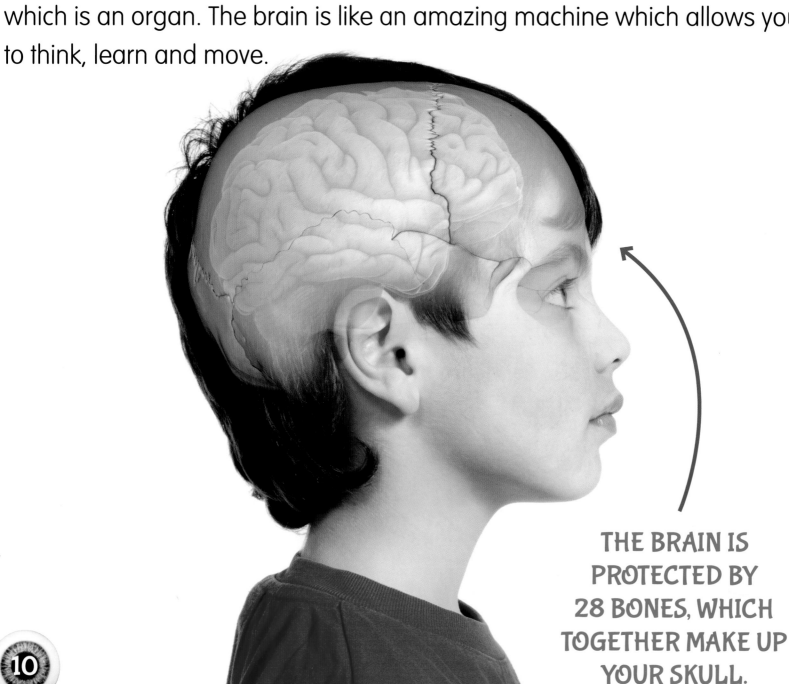

THE BRAIN IS PROTECTED BY 28 BONES, WHICH TOGETHER MAKE UP YOUR SKULL.

Your face has two eyes, a mouth and a nose. There are over 40 muscles in your face. You can use these muscles to move your face so you can chew your food, open your eyes and even to show how you are feeling.

HOW MANY FUNNY FACES CAN YOU PULL?

BODY

Your whole body is covered in skin. It protects the inside of your body from harmful germs. It can repair itself when it gets damaged or hurt. Your skin also gives you the **sense** of touch.

SKIN IS OUR BIGGEST ORGAN AND IT IS WATERPROOF!

Inside the centre of your body are many important organs, such as the lungs and heart. The heart pumps blood around the whole of the body. It is important to keep your heart healthy by exercising and keeping a healthy **diet**.

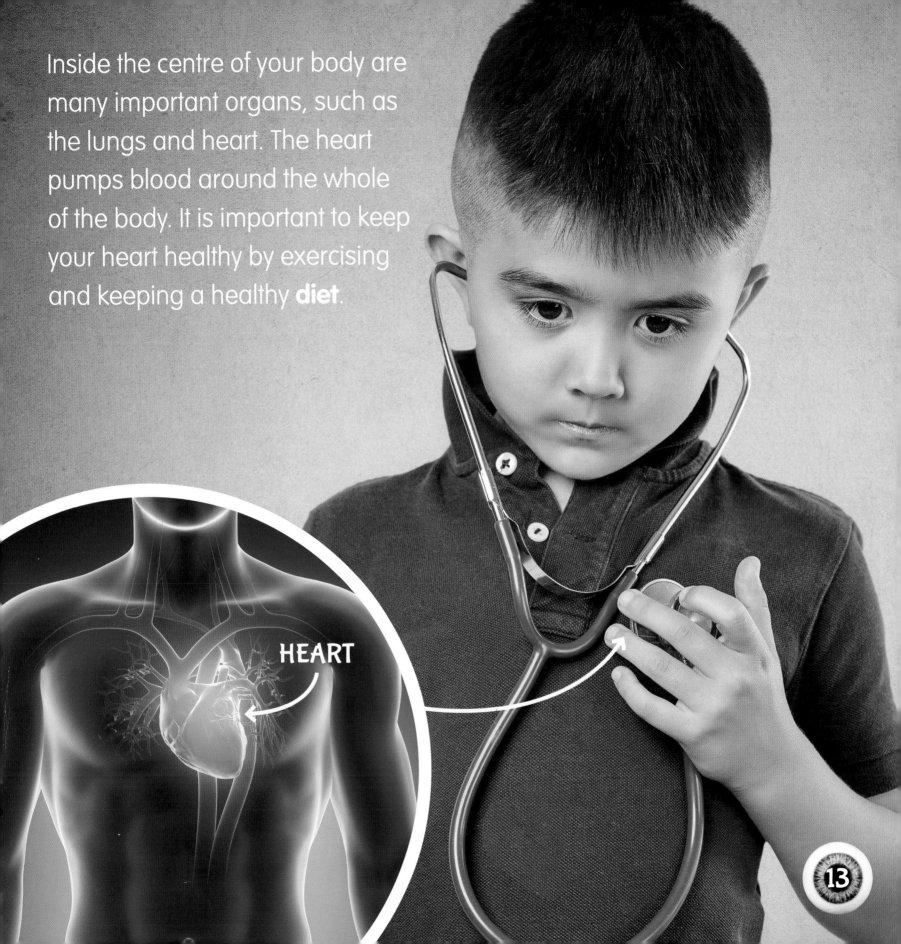

HEART

LEGS AND FEET

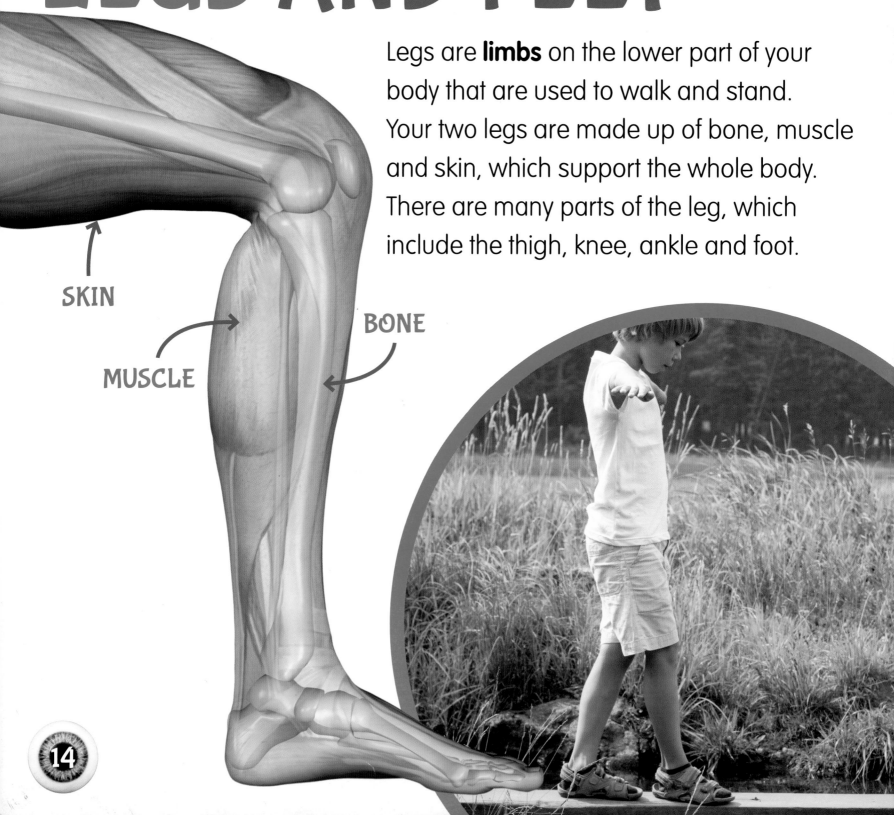

Legs are **limbs** on the lower part of your body that are used to walk and stand. Your two legs are made up of bone, muscle and skin, which support the whole body. There are many parts of the leg, which include the thigh, knee, ankle and foot.

SKIN

MUSCLE

BONE

The foot is connected to the end of the leg and has 26 small bones. There are five toes on each foot which help you to balance and give support for walking, running and jumping.

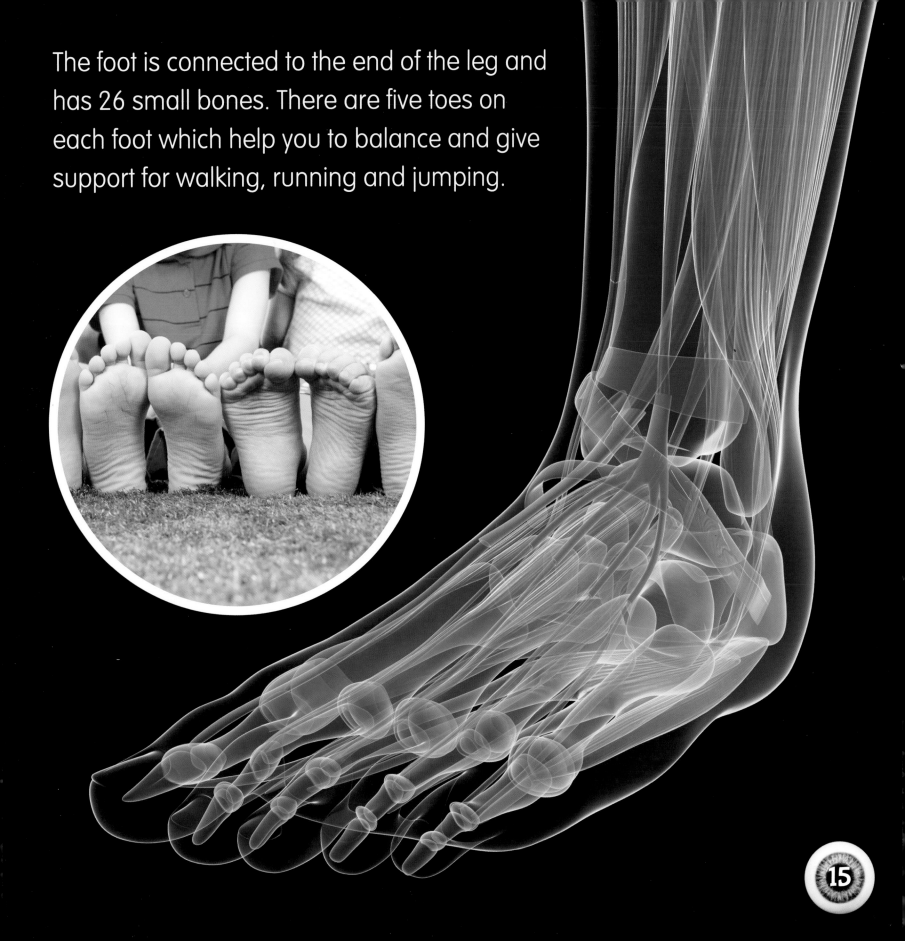

ARMS AND HANDS

You have two arms that are connected to your body by your shoulders. Like legs, they are made up of bones and muscles and are covered in skin. You can use your arms to reach out so that you can touch and feel things with your hands.

The elbow is the main **joint** in your arm which allows it to bend. Hands are connected to your arms by wrists. Each hand has 27 bones and many joints. You can use your hands to hold and touch things.

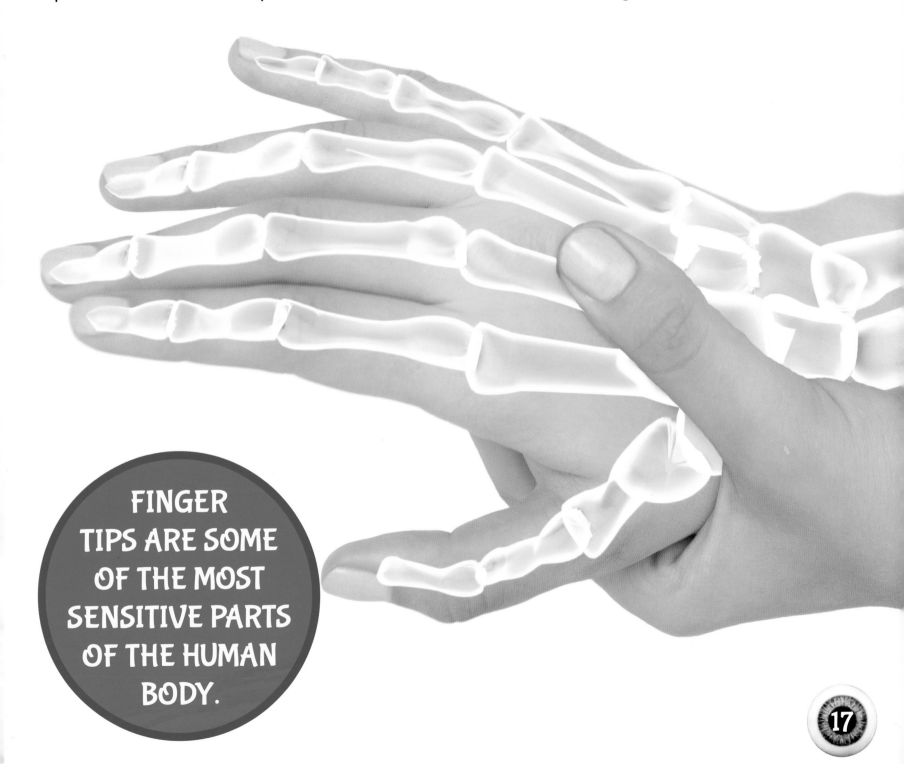

FINGER TIPS ARE SOME OF THE MOST SENSITIVE PARTS OF THE HUMAN BODY.

EYES AND EARS

You have two eyes and two ears. They are used to see and hear the world around you. Your eyes allow you to see shapes and colours. Your eyes are protected by eyelids and eyelashes, which help to keep the dust and dirt out.

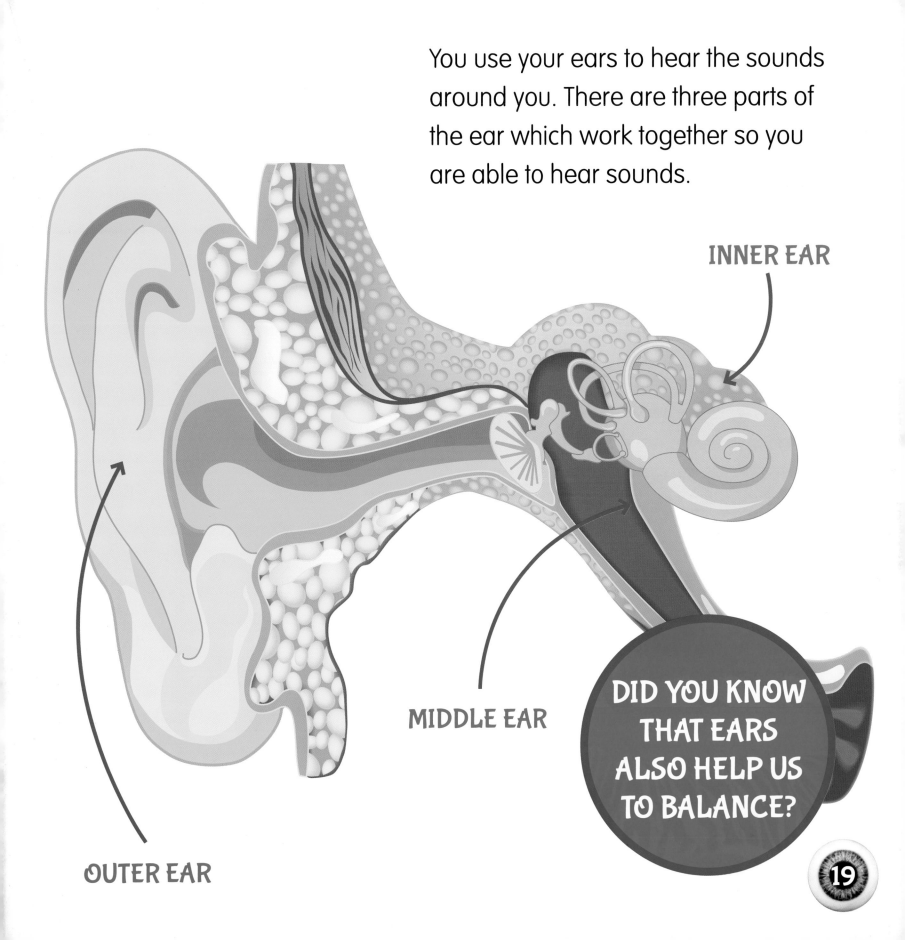

You use your ears to hear the sounds around you. There are three parts of the ear which work together so you are able to hear sounds.

INNER EAR

MIDDLE EAR

OUTER EAR

DID YOU KNOW THAT EARS ALSO HELP US TO BALANCE?

MOUTH AND NOSE

You use your mouth to breathe, eat and taste. Inside the mouth are teeth and a tongue. Your teeth are used to chew food so that it can be swallowed. Your tongue is covered in tiny **taste buds**, which allow you to taste different types of food.

TASTE BUDS

You can also breathe through your nose. As you breathe through your nose, it sends signals to your brain, which will let you know what you are smelling.

WHAT IS YOUR FAVOURITE SMELL?

LET'S EXPERIMENT!

Do you know how important your sense of touch is?
Let's find out!

You will need:

BLINDFOLD

ORANGE

CUCUMBER

APPLE

BANANA

TOMATO

TOP TIP
- - - - - - -
ASK AN ADULT TO HELP YOU!

Step 1

Place the fruit and vegetables in front of you and then place the blindfold over your eyes.

Step 2

Pick up one of the items in front of you. How does it feel? Is it rough or smooth? What shape is it?

Step 3

Take off your blindfold … were you right?

Step 4

Have another go!

Results:

Your experiment will show you how you can sense the things around you by touch.

GLOSSARY

body tissue	what organs and other body parts are made of
diet	types of food that a human or animal eats
joint	a place where two or more bones meet
limbs	legs and arms
organs	parts of the body that have particular jobs to do
taste buds	tiny sensors on the tongue and the inside of the mouth, which allow the sense of taste
tendons	long, stringy cords that join muscle to bones
sense	one of the five senses including sight, smell, touch, taste and hearing

INDEX